PROPERTY
ELEMENTARY SCHOOL LIBRARIES
OAK PARK, ILLINOIS

MANN MEDIA CENTER

Gift of the
Mann School
P.T.O.

Great Artists
Andy Warhol

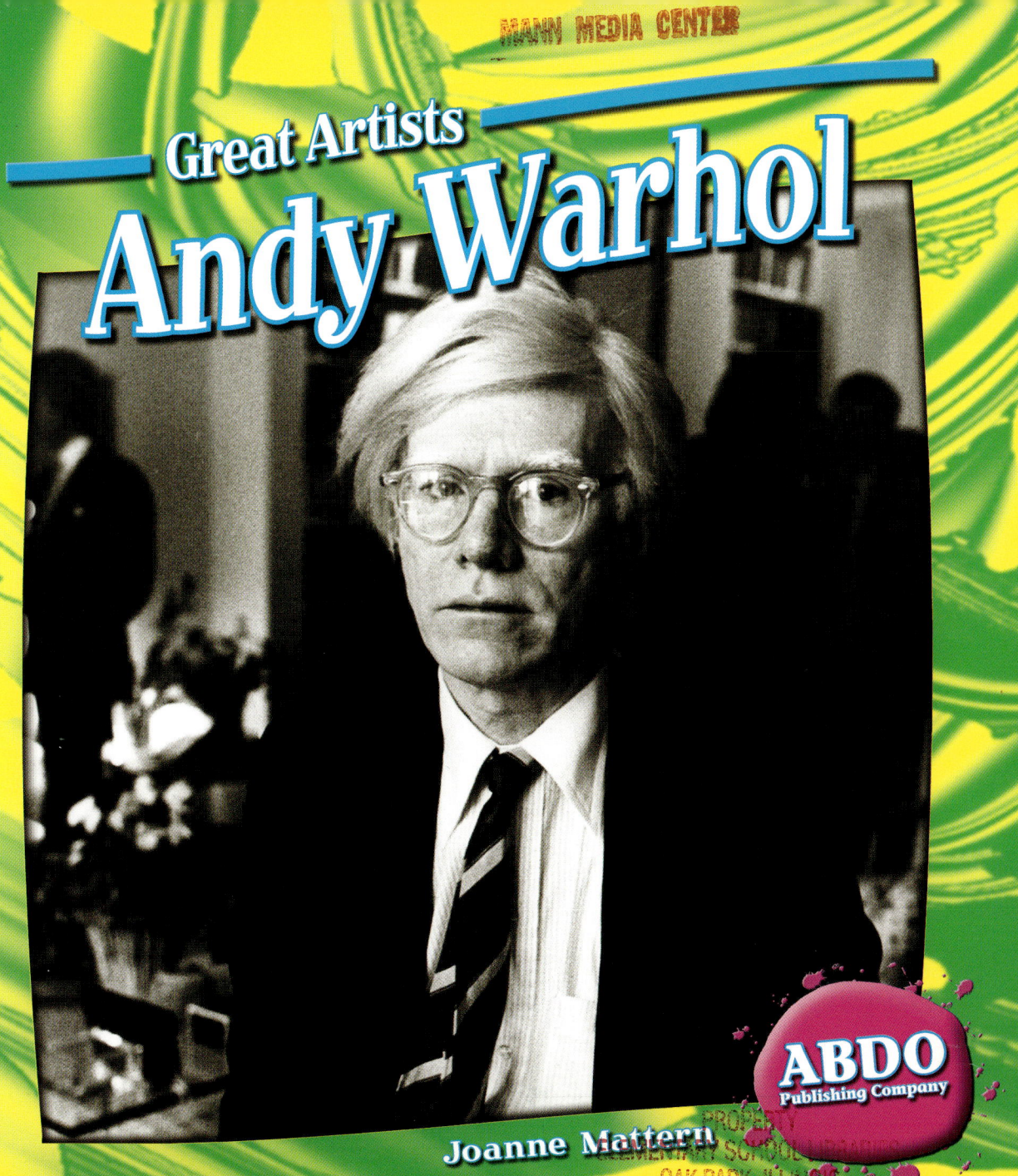

Joanne Mattern

ABDO Publishing Company

visit us at
www.abdopub.com

Published by ABDO Publishing Company, 4940 Viking Drive, Edina, Minnesota 55435. Copyright © 2005 by Abdo Consulting Group, Inc. International copyrights reserved in all countries. No part of this book may be reproduced in any form without written permission from the publisher. The Checkerboard Library™ is a trademark and logo of ABDO Publishing Company.

Printed in the United States.

Cover Photo: Getty Images
Interior Photos: Corbis pp. 9, 11, 13, 14, 15, 16, 19, 20, 24, 26, 27, 29; Getty Images pp. 1, 5, 17, 21, 22, 23, 25; © The Andy Warhol Foundation for the Visual Arts

Series Coordinator: Megan Murphy
Editors: Jennifer R. Krueger, Megan Murphy
Cover Design: Neil Klinepier
Interior Design: Dave Bullen

Library of Congress Cataloging-in-Publication Data

Mattern, Joanne, 1963-
 Andy Warhol / Joanne Mattern.
   p. cm. -- (Great artists)
 Includes index.
 ISBN 1-59197-850-5
 1. Warhol, Andy, 1928---Juvenile literature. 2. Artists--United States--Biography--Juvenile literature. I. Title.

N6537.W28M38 2005
700'.92--dc22
[B]
                                                                    2004052812

Contents

Andy Warhol 4
Timeline 6
Fun Facts 7
A Humble Start 8
A Sickly Child 10
Art School 12
A New Name 14
Success 16
Redefining Art 18
Repetition 20
The Factory 22
Valerie Solanas 24
Celebrity 26
Pop Art Legend 28
Glossary 30
Saying It 31
Web Sites 31
Index 32

Andy Warhol

Andy Warhol is a popular American **print** artist. He helped create a style of art called Pop Art. Warhol painted pictures of ordinary objects. He also painted famous people. He used bright colors and simple shapes. His art is fun to look at.

Warhol did most of his painting during the 1960s. This was an exciting time in popular **culture**. New kinds of music, literature, art, and movies were being created. This inspired Warhol to look at art in a new way. He made other people see it in a new way, too.

Warhol's art showed what was popular in American culture. It was different from anything that had been created before. Many people did not take his work seriously. But, many more saw that he was making art fun and easy for anyone to understand.

Andy Warhol in 1981

Timeline

1928 ~ Andrew Warhola was born on August 6 in Pittsburgh, Pennsylvania.

1932 ~ Warhol started school. However, he was bullied by one of his classmates on the first day and did not go back for two years.

1945 to 1949 ~ Warhol attended the Carnegie Institute of Technology.

1957 ~ Warhol won the Art Director's Club Medal for his advertising work.

1962 ~ Warhol painted *32 Campbell's Soup Cans*.

1964 ~ Warhol exhibited *Brillo Boxes*.

1968 ~ On June 3, Warhol was shot by an actress who appeared in one of his movies.

1978 ~ Warhol started his own magazine called *Interview*.

1987 ~ On February 22, Warhol died after suffering a heart attack.

Fun Facts

- Andy Warhol is famous for saying, "In the future, everyone will be world-famous for 15 minutes."

- In 1957, Warhol had plastic surgery to change the shape of his nose. He had also lost most of his hair by the time he was 25. He wore wigs for the rest of his life.

- The Warhol Family Museum of Modern Art was established in 1991 in Slovakia, a country in Eastern Europe, near the birthplace of Warhol's parents.

- Warhol said that he started Pop Art because he hated Abstract Expressionism. Abstract Expressionists did not use recognizable images. Instead, they used color and motion to show ideas or feelings. Abstract Expressionism had dominated the art scene up until the 1950s.

A Humble Start

Andrew Warhola was born on August 6, 1928, in Pittsburgh, Pennsylvania. He was the youngest of three boys. Andy's parents were Andrej and Julia. They were **immigrants** from Czechoslovakia, a country in Europe.

Like many immigrants, the Warholas were very poor. They lived in a tiny house with no indoor plumbing. Andy's father worked in a coal mine. His mother cleaned houses. She also made metal flowers out of tin cans and sold them for extra money.

Andy started school when he was four. On his first day at school, one of his classmates hit him. Andy asked his mother to let him stay home. Julia agreed, and Andy did not go back to school for two years. Instead, he stayed home with his mother. The two drew pictures and read stories together.

A Sickly Child

Andy was often sick as a child. When he was eight years old, he **contracted** a serious disease called **rheumatic fever**. Then he caught another disease called **chorea**. The chorea made Andy's body shake. He had to stay in bed for a month until it went away.

Later, Andy developed a strange skin condition. His skin became very pale and had red blotches. Andy's skin stayed this way for the rest of his life.

Andy missed a lot of school because he was sick so often. But, he did not mind staying home. He watched cartoons. And, his mother gave him coloring books and books of paper dolls. Every time Andy finished a page in his coloring book, his mother gave him a chocolate bar.

Andy also enjoyed reading movie magazines. These magazines were full of pictures of famous movie stars. He later used images from old cartoons and movies in his art.

Images from Warhol's childhood appear often in his artwork. Cartoon characters were some of his favorite subjects.

Art School

Andy was a good student even though he missed many days of school because of his illnesses. When Andy was 14, his father died. The family discovered that Andrej had carefully saved enough money for Andy to go to college.

In 1945, Andy entered the Carnegie Institute of Technology in Pittsburgh. He had trouble keeping up with his studies. But he liked his art classes. His artwork was so good that his art teachers gave him extra help.

Andy also went to school during the summer. He spent many hours drawing pictures of his neighborhood. He painted the hardworking **immigrants** who lived there. Andy's paintings won a prize and were exhibited at a Carnegie art show.

Andy liked to draw using a style called blotted line. First, he drew a picture on a piece of paper. Next, he traced the image

Statues at the Carnegie Institute in Pittsburgh

with wet ink. Then, he pressed another piece of paper onto the wet image to make a copy. The copy looked smudged because the ink didn't soak evenly into the paper.

A New Name

While he was at school, Andy worked at a Pittsburgh department store. He painted backgrounds for the window displays. His boss at the store often gave Andy fashion magazines to read. He admired the stylish models and clothes in these magazines.

Andy dreamed of going to New York City and becoming part of the fashion world. In 1949, he graduated from Carnegie. Then, he packed his things and moved to New York.

A few days after he arrived, Andy met the art director of *Glamour* magazine.

Warhol created these female fashion figures for magazine advertisements.

Glamour featured many articles about movie stars and fashion. The art director gave Andy a job drawing shoes.

Andy did a good job, and *Glamour* published his drawings. But, his last name was accidentally printed as "Warhol," not "Warhola." Andy did not mind. From then on, he went by Andy Warhol.

A Life Savers advertisement Warhol created in 1985

Success

Warhol became a very successful **commercial artist**. His drawings appeared in many fashion magazines. He amazed people with his energy and determination. Warhol would often stay up all night working. In 1957, Warhol won the Art Director's Club Medal for his work.

Warhol made a lot of money. But, he still dressed in torn, sloppy clothes. His friends called him "Raggedy Andy." He also continued to share apartments with other artists.

When Warhol finally bought his own place, his mother came to live with him. Their house was messy and cluttered. Warhol and his mother slept on mattresses on the floor.

Warhol liked drawing cats. In fact, he had about 20 cats in his apartment.

> Warhol always had a close relationship with his mother. Even after he became famous, Julia lived with him in his town house in New York City.

Warhol went to Catholic Mass almost every morning. After Mass, he would work or visit art directors and magazine offices. Warhol also went out almost every night. He liked to go to the theater and parties. Even though Warhol liked to be social, he was shy and did not talk very much.

Redefining Art

Other **commercial artists** admired Warhol. But, many in the **fine arts** did not consider him to be a real artist. This upset Warhol. He wanted people to think of him as a real artist, not just a magazine illustrator.

In the early 1960s, Warhol began painting ordinary objects. He painted a picture of a soda bottle that was six feet (2 m) tall! Warhol also painted characters from old cartoon movies. He would project a slide onto a piece of **canvas**. Then, he would paint over the slide to create a picture.

The type of art Warhol created was called Pop Art. Many other artists were also experimenting with Pop Art. Warhol began showing his work at galleries. Some people hated his pictures of ordinary objects. Other people loved them. Either way, people began to notice his work.

Pop Art displays images of popular culture and society. Pop artists use well-known brands and famous people as their subjects, such as this Cabbage Patch Kids doll.

Repetition

Warhol liked to paint many pictures of the same thing. In 1962, a famous actress named Marilyn Monroe died. That same year, Warhol painted a series of pictures of her.

Later that year, a friend suggested Warhol paint something that was so common, people did not see it as art. Warhol loved to eat soup. So, he decided to paint cans of Campbell's Soup.

There were many flavors of Campbell's Soup made at that time. Warhol bought all the different kinds. Then, he spent hours copying the cans on a white background. He painted the cans 32 times on one **canvas**! Each can was slightly different from the next.

Warhol called this piece *32 Campbell's Soup Cans*. The painting became very famous. Warhol also repeated images of many other objects, such as *Five Coke Bottles*.

In his Marilyn Monroe series, Warhol used the same photograph. But, he changed the colors of each image.

20   Great Artists

Artist's Corner

Andy Warhol

Warhol created many paintings using a process called photographic silk screening. A silk screen is a sheet of framed mesh that allows ink or paint through it. To make a print, Warhol placed a photographic image on a silk screen over a piece of canvas. Then, he painted over the screen. The paint passed through the screen and onto the canvas underneath. This transferred the image onto the canvas.

The paintings looked very much alike, but they were a little different from each other, too. Warhol often changed colors and made many versions of the same image. Warhol could make a lot of paintings in a short amount of time. For example, Warhol produced many versions of the Campbell's Soup can, but the cans were never exactly the same.

32 Campbell's Soup Cans

The Factory

Warhol's silk screening process and repeated images were creating so much work that he needed help. So, he hired assistants to help him paint. They worked at Warhol's art studio. Warhol called his studio the Factory.

Warhol also created sculptures in his studio. Like his paintings, his sculptures were often common objects. In 1964, he exhibited a series of wooden crates that looked like boxes of Brillo pads. The piece was called *Brillo Boxes*. The next year he completed another box sculpture, *Campbell's Tomato Juice*.

Warhol was interested in making movies, too. He set up a camera and filmed people doing ordinary things.

Brillo Boxes

One film was titled *Sleep*. Warhol recorded a man sleeping for six hours. Another film was called *Eat*. It showed a man eating a mushroom.

Other films showed Warhol's friends sitting around or talking to each other. Some people hated Warhol's movies. Other people praised Warhol for showing life as it really was.

Warhol did most of his work at the Factory. Here, he is working on the Campbell's Tomato Juice *sculpture in 1964.*

Valerie Solanas

Warhol had many friends and admirers. The Factory was always full of artists, actors, musicians, and other creative people. But not everyone liked Warhol.

A woman named Valerie Solanas had appeared in one of Warhol's movies. She was mentally ill and wanted Warhol to pay more attention to her. On June 3, 1968, Solanas walked into the Factory. She shot Warhol in the stomach.

Warhol was rushed to the hospital. Doctors performed an emergency operation to save his life. For more than a week, Warhol's condition was critical. He finally began to recover. But, he had to stay in the hospital for six weeks. Solanas was sent to jail.

Actress Valerie Solanas (center) *was arrested for shooting Andy Warhol and an art dealer.*

Great Artists

After the shooting, Warhol did not want to be around people he did not know. He also set limits on who was allowed at the Factory.

Celebrity

Warhol was even more shy and cautious after the shooting. However, he still loved to go to parties. During the 1970s, he went out almost every night. Warhol was always surrounded by famous actresses, rock stars, and other celebrities.

By now, Warhol had become a celebrity himself. Photographs of him appeared in magazines. Warhol was invited to the White House several times. He painted a portrait of President Jimmy Carter for the cover of *New York Times* magazine.

Warhol was doing other kinds of work as well. In 1978, he started his own magazine. It was called *Interview*. It featured interviews

Warhol holding a copy of Interview

Albert Einstein

of his famous friends. Warhol started writing books, too. His most famous book is called *POPism: The Warhol Sixties*. It is **transcripts** of his diary entries.

Warhol also began portrait painting. He painted portraits of famous people, such as Albert Einstein. His portraits sold for thousands of dollars. They were exhibited in art museums around the world.

All this hard work made Warhol a wealthy man. Shopping was one of Warhol's favorite things to do. He went out every day with an envelope full of money. Warhol liked to go to flea markets and **antique** stores. He bought anything he liked.

Pop Art Legend

Warhol continued to paint, write, and create art until 1987. Early that year, he began having terrible pains in his stomach. A doctor said his **gallbladder** was **infected**. Warhol had to have an operation to have it removed.

On February 21, Warhol had the operation. Everything went well. But the next morning, a nurse found Warhol had died after suffering a heart attack during the night. He was buried in Pittsburgh, near the graves of his mother and father.

At the time of his death, Warhol was one of the richest artists in America. He had about $100 million. Warhol never married or had children. Most of his money was used to start a foundation to promote the visual arts.

Today, Andy Warhol is remembered as one of the most important American artists. He helped make Pop Art important and popular around the world. For the first time, people realized that cartoons, movie stars, and soup cans could be art.

Warhol created Self-Portrait *in 1986.*

Glossary

antique - an old item that has collectible value.
canvas - a piece of cloth that is framed and used as a surface for a painting.
chorea - a disorder of the nervous system that affects movement and coordination.
commercial artist - an artist who does work for businesses rather than galleries.
contract - to become affected with, as in a disease or virus.
culture - the customs, arts, and tools of a nation or people at a certain time.
fine art - art that focuses on the creation of beautiful objects.
gallbladder - an internal organ that stores fluid from the liver.
immigrate - to enter another country to live. A person who immigrates is called an immigrant.
infect - to invade an individual or organ with a disease-producing agent.
print - a reproduction of an original work of art.
rheumatic fever - a disease that occurs mainly in children. It is characterized by fever and pain in the joints and especially in the lungs.
transcript - a written, printed, or typed copy.

Great Artists

Carnegie - KAHR-nuh-gee
chorea - ku-REE-uh
Czechoslovakia - chehk-uh-sloh-VAHK-ee-uh
rheumatic - ru-MA-tihk
Warhol - WAWR-hawl

To learn more about Andy Warhol, visit ABDO Publishing Company on the World Wide Web at **www.abdopub.com**. Web sites about Warhol are featured on our Book Links page. These links are routinely monitored and updated to provide the most current information available.

Index

A
awards 12, 16
B
Brillo Boxes 22
C
Campbell's Tomato Juice 22
Carnegie Institute of Technology 12, 14
Carter, Jimmy 26
Czechoslovakia 8
E
education 8, 10, 12, 14
Einstein, Albert 27

F
Factory 22, 24
family 8, 10, 12, 16, 28
filmmaker 22, 23, 24
Five Coke Bottles 20
G
Glamour magazine 14
I
illnesses 10, 12, 28
Interview magazine 26, 27
M
Monroe, Marilyn 20

N
New York City, New York 14
New York Times magazine 26
P
Pittsburgh, Pennsylvania 8, 12, 14, 28
Pop Art 4, 18, 28
POPism: The Warhol Sixties 27
S
Solanas, Valerie 24
T
32 Campbell's Soup Cans 20